Walt Disney's Donald Duck in An Easter Basketcase

"ISN'T THIS JUST *SWELL*, DONALD? TO BE OUT HERE AMONGST THE PEOPLE, ALL ENJOYING THE ANNUAL *DUCKBURG EASTER PARADE?*"

D 2004-132

"THE WARM *SHARING* IN THAT WHICH BINDS US ALL! IT'S TIMES LIKE THESE THAT REMIND US TO SHED ALL OUR PETTY PRIVATE SHELLS..."

"...TO BE *ONE* WITH FAMILY AND FRIENDS...TO *APPRECIATE* EACH OTHER'S *COMPANY!*"

"*YOURS* IN PARTICULAR! I AM *SO* PROUD OF YOU! TOO OFTEN..."

"EXCUSE ME, DAISY..."

"...COULD YOU *TONE IT DOWN?* I'M TRYING TO FOLLOW THE *BALLGAME!*"

"...*CAUGHT* BY GREENBERG ON THIRD!"

HEY!

WHAT?!

THAT!

DAISY'S POETRY BOOK HAS BEEN *STEADYING* YOUR WORKBENCH FOR MONTHS!

THAT'S WHAT WE WERE *TRYING* TO SAY!

EITHER YOU *FORGOT...*

...OR YOU CAN'T *HANDLE* THE *TRUTH!*

EITHER WAY, WE THINK YOU SHOULD *APOLOGIZE* TO AUNT DAISY!

BOYS...

FETCH YOUR *EASTER BASKETS!* I'LL WHIP UP A BATCH OF *EASTER EGGS* SO WE CAN *HONOR* DAISY'S INVITE AFTER ALL!

Soon—

ON THE PHONE... ...AUNT DAISY SOUNDED SO *RELIEVED...*

...THAT YOU'VE *REPENTED,* UNCA DONALD!

OH, I'M SO *EXCITED* YOU'VE COME! I'VE SET UP REFRESHMENTS IN THE BACKYARD, BUT WE SHOULD *HIDE* OUR EGGS FIRST!

AS I SAID, IT'S DAYS LIKE THESE THAT BRING US *CLOSER TOGETHER!* THEY'RE TOO *RARE* TO WASTE *ARGUING!*

AGAIN, DAISY...MY SINCERE APOLOGIES!

ENOUGH SAID, DONALD! LET'S JUST GRAB OUR BASKETS AND GET ON WITH THE *EGG HUNT!*

?

UNCA DONALD NEVER SAID ANYTHING ABOUT *RETURNING* THAT BOOK!

AND WHY DID HE *HIDE* IT IN HIS BASKET?

LET'S FOLLOW HIM!

SOMETHING IS UP!

AND REMEMBER DONALD, THERE ARE *NO LOSERS* TODAY! TEE-HEE!

IF HE WANTS TO FIND AS *MANY* EGGS AS POSSIBLE, WHY IS HE *STICKING CLOSE* TO DAISY?

I *FOUND* MY FIRST ONE!

FOUND *ANOTHER ONE* HERE!

WHAT DOES HE EXPECT TO FIND ON ON TOP OF THE *BOOKCASE?*

I *GET IT!*

HE'S GOING TO *PLANT* THE BOOK THERE AND *FEIGN* HAVING *FOUND* IT UNDER HER VERY NOSE!

HE'S GOING TO *SHAME* HER INTO THINKING SHE WAS *WRONG* AFTER ALL!

SHE HAS A POINT! SHE'LL ONLY "FIND" THE BOOK AS LONG AS SHE *KEEPS LOOKING* FOR MORE EGGS!

I GUESS THE KIDS ARE *ON* TO ME! AN EXTRA *COMPLICATION* TO TAKE CARE OF...

...BY *SACRIFICING* THE TWO EXTRA EGGS I *POCKETED* TO GIVE ME AN *EDGE* IN THE HUNT! HEH-HEH!

WHATEVER IT TAKES, WE'LL *CONTINUE* TO LURE AUNT DAISY *AWAY* FROM UNCA DONALD!

THREE OF OUR EGGS *AREN'T* TOO BIG A PRICE!

HEY! OVER *THERE!*

SEEMS A GOOD EASTER DEED NEVER GOES *UNREWARDED!*

TWO! FOR THE *TAKING!*

GROW UP, BOYS!

PUSH!

YOU'RE SO LAUGHABLY *GULLIBLE!* REAL LIFE ONLY DEALS YOU HANDS THAT SHOVE YOU DOWN A *RAT HOLE!*

CLICK!

MAYBE *YOU,* UNCA DONALD...

...BUT DON'T TAKE IT OUT ON *AUNT DAISY!*

AND LET US *OUT* OF *THIS* RAT HOLE!

BOM

BAM

NOT UNTIL I SEE HER COME FACE TO FACE WITH THAT BOOK OF POEMS IN HER *OWN* HOME! THAT'LL *STOP* HER FROM PUSHING ME AROUND!

I *SACRIFICED* MY BALLGAME TICKET TO GO TO THE PARADE WITH HER! FOR YEARS I'VE HAD TO BEND OVER *BACKWARDS* TO *ACCOMMODATE HER!*

IT'S TIME TO *DRAW THE LINE*, AND HOW BETTER THAN BY LEAVING HER WITH *EGG ON HER FACE?!*

AND HOW *APPROPRIATE* TO PICK *EASTER* FOR THAT!

ALL THE BOYS' EGGS JUST PROVE THAT LOOKING OUT FOR *NUMBER ONE* MAKES THINGS COME YOUR WAY! HEH-HEH!

OH, *DONALD! KIDS!* WRAP IT UP AND COME JOIN ME IN THE YARD!

SHE'S *CALLING OFF* THE HUNT?!

YEAH, AND WITH IT YOUR CHANCE TO BE *SNEAKY!!*

WHATEVER HIS NEXT MOVE IS, IT'LL HAVE TO BE *DESPERATE!*

IT'S USUALLY *NOT* A PRETTY SIGHT WHEN UNCA DONALD GETS DESPERATE!

WE *MUST* FIND A WAY OUT OF HERE AND *STOP* HIM!

BY THE WAY, *WHERE* ARE WE?

HEY! WHAT'S THIS?

MY, LOOK AT YOUR BASKET! I'M SO GLAD TO SEE YOU *ENJOYING* YOURSELF! BUT WHERE ARE THE *BOYS?*

UH...WELL...YOU KNOW *KIDS!* THEY JUST DON'T KNOW WHEN ENOUGH IS ENOUGH...HEH-HEH!

MIGHT AS WELL START FILLING THEIR GLASSES!

I NEED A GOOD SPOT!

HM...IT LACKS *SUBTLETY,* BUT WHY NOT *HERE!*

IT'S A *CHUTE!*

THIS USED TO BE A *COAL CELLAR!*

UNLESS IT'S *PAD-LOCKED* ON THE OUTSIDE, IT'S OUR *WAY OUT!*

NOT *TOO* FAR FETCHED TO ASSUME A BOOK CAN BE USED TO *BAR* A DOOR!

CAN'T REACH THE DOORS... THIS RAMP IS TOO *SLIPPERY!*

HERE! WE CAN USE *THIS!*

SO AS NOT TO IMPLICATE *MYSELF,* I'D BETTER PUT SOME DISTANCE—

DONALD, *LOOK OUT!* MY *EGGS!*

BUMP

WUP

WUP

WUP

!

≈PHEW!≈ NONE OF THEM *BROKE!*

SOMETHING *SOFT* IS JAMMING THE DOORS!

WUP

WUP

A *FIRM HEAVE-HO* WILL FIX THAT!

CLIMB DOWN AND LET'S USE THE *LADDER!*

≈ULP!≈ THAT'S WHERE I LOCKED UP THE *BOYS!*

TEE-HEE! I HOPE YOU WEREN'T SO *NAUGHTY* AS TO BELIEVE YOU CAN WIN THE HUNT *THIS* WAY, DONALD!

THE BOOK'S *SLIPPING!* BETTER PUT IT BACK IN THE BASKET AND WAIT THIS OUT!

WUP

WUP

ON THREE! *ONE!*

TWO!

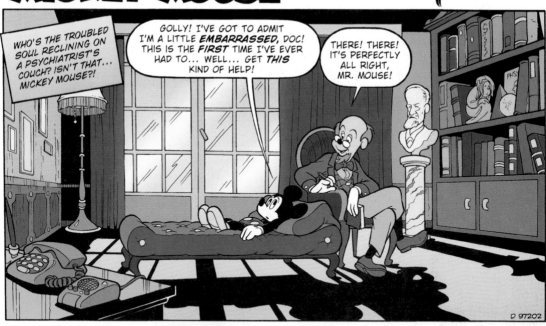

WHO'S THE TROUBLED SOUL RECLINING ON A PSYCHIATRIST'S COUCH? ISN'T THAT... MICKEY MOUSE?!

GOLLY! I'VE GOT TO ADMIT I'M A LITTLE *EMBARRASSED*, DOC! THIS IS THE *FIRST* TIME I'VE EVER HAD TO... WELL... GET *THIS* KIND OF HELP!

THERE! THERE! IT'S PERFECTLY ALL RIGHT, MR. MOUSE!

D 97202

I ASSURE YOU, THERE'S *NOTHING* TO BE ASHAMED OF! *EVERYONE* CAN USE A KINDLY EAR TO TELL THEIR TROUBLES TO!

I HAVEN'T MENTIONED MY PROBLEM TO *ANYONE!* THE THING IS... I DON'T WANT YOU TO GET THE IDEA...THAT IS... I'M *NOT CRAZY!*

I *THINK!*

OF *COURSE* YOU'RE NOT, MR. MOUSE! WHY DON'T YOU JUST *RELAX* AND RELATE WHAT'S BOTHERING YOU?

⇥ULP!⇤ WELL, OKAY!

LET ME TELL YOU ALL ABOUT THE *IMP AND I...*

"BACK AT HOME, I TOOK A CLOSER LOOK AT THE JAR! IT WAS HALF-FILLED WITH A THICK, GOOEY, BLACK SUBSTANCE—"

I HOPE I CAN CLEAN THAT STUFF OUT OF THERE! BUT FIRST, I'LL POLISH UP THE *OUTSIDE*!

GOSH! THERE'S A STRANGE *INSCRIPTION* ON THE GLASS! WHAT'S IT SAY? *"ROT IN A JAR OF TAR"*?!

"AND THAT'S WHEN MY *TROUBLES* BEGAN!"

HUH?

PHOOMPH!

GREETINGS, MOUSY MORTAL!

≈GASP!≈ AM I SEEING THINGS? WHO, OR *WHAT*, ARE *YOU*?!

ISN'T IT *OBVIOUS*? I'M A RESIDENT OF THE *ELEVENTH DIMENSION*! LONG AGO I DISCOVERED A WAY OF CROSSING OVER TO *THIS* VIBRATORY PLANE!

I LIKE TO THINK OF YOUR WORLD AS MY OWN *PRIVATE PLAYGROUND*!

HEH! THAT'S NICE! BUH-BUH BUT WOULDN'T YOU *RATHER* GO BACK IN *HERE* WHERE IT'S *SNUG* AND *COMFY*?

BAH! THAT SMELLY JAR WAS A *PRISON*! I WANT IT TO *GO AWAY*!

POOF!

"I DID, AND—"

HUH?

HEY! YOU! IT'S ME, YOU MAGICAL MIDGET! FACE FRONT!

YOU'VE GONE TOO FAR THIS TIME, SHORT STUFF!

WHAT ARE YOU TALKING ABOUT, BARE-TAILED ONE?

I'M REFERRING TO THE SHENANIGANS YOU PULLED IN THAT ALLEY, FELLAH!

YOUR IMAGINATION MUST BE IN OVERDRIVE! I'VE DONE NOTHING IN THERE!

OH YEAH?!

IF THAT ISN'T ONE OF YOUR MAGICAL PRANKS, THEN I'M THE KING OF BULGARIA!

BUT I'M INNOCENT!

THEN WHAT DO YOU CALL THAT?!

HUH? WHY, THAT LOOKS LIKE A... A... RAT FOR A JANITOR?!?

FROOMPH!

HA! I GOT YOU! YOU SAID THE INSCRIPTION BACKWARDS! SO LONG, SUCKER!

NO FAIR! YOU TRICKED ME! BUT JUST WAIT! I'LL BE BACK!

"SO THAT'S THE STORY, DOC!"

WITH THE IMP GONE, EVERY-THING WENT BACK TO *NORMAL!* THE BUILDINGS! THE OLD MAN! GOOFY! *EVERYTHING!* AND NOBODY BUT *ME* HAD ANY MEMORY OF THE WEIRD GOINGS-ON!

AND NOW A *YEAR* HAS ELAPSED! THE IMP MIGHT SHOW UP *ANY MINUTE!* I'VE BEEN *DREADING* HIS RETURN! YOU GOTTA LEVEL WITH ME, DOC — AM I *NUTS?!*

TUT-TUT! YOU'RE *NOT* CRAZY! AND I WOULDN'T WORRY IF I WERE YOU!

NO?

WHAT YOU HAD WAS A *BAD DREAM!* A HYPER-REAL *NIGHTMARE!* THEY CAN BE *QUITE* CONVINCING, BUT YOU'VE BEEN *FRETTING* A WHOLE YEAR FOR *NO REASON!*

GEE, I GUESS YOU'RE *RIGHT!* AND FINALLY TELLING SOMEONE ABOUT IT MAKES ME FEEL *A WHOLE LOT BETTER!*

THANKS, DOC! YOU'RE A *SWELL* GUY! SO LONG!

GOOD-BYE, MR. MOUSE!

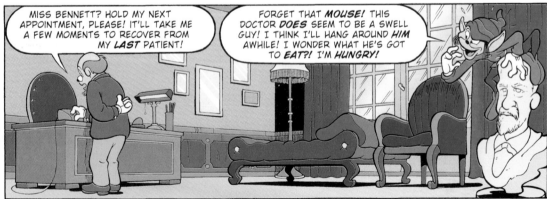

MISS BENNETT? HOLD MY NEXT APPOINTMENT, PLEASE! IT'LL TAKE ME A FEW MOMENTS TO RECOVER FROM MY *LAST* PATIENT!

FORGET THAT *MOUSE!* THIS DOCTOR *DOES* SEEM TO BE A SWELL GUY! I THINK I'LL HANG AROUND *HIM* AWHILE! I WONDER WHAT HE'S GOT TO *EAT?!* I'M *HUNGRY!*

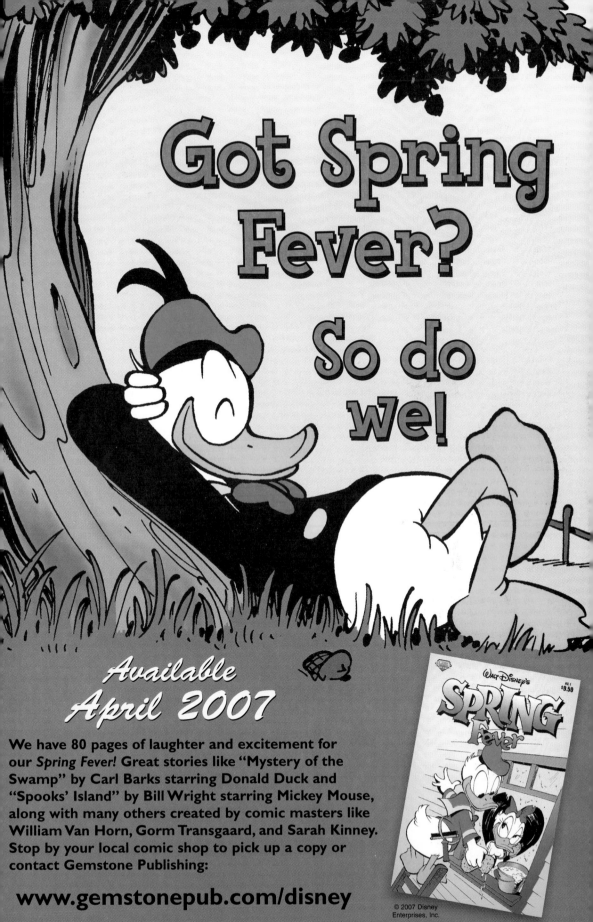

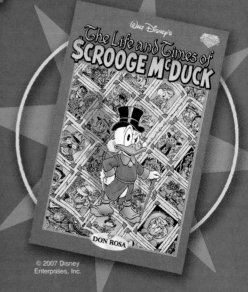

WALT DISNEY'S SCAMP Son of LADY and the TRAMP

YX 55-10-31

After Tramp and Lady got married, of course they didn't "live happily ever after!"..

Sometimes they disagreed...

CAMP LADY

Sometimes they sulked...

...and did they have problems!

All the puppies were problems!

Tramp! Make them behave!

Aw, let 'em wander--- they'll come back!

The toughest problem was Scamp.

I won't come back!

Scamp was gentle like his mother...

He was inquisitive like his father...

BUT HE WAS STILL JUST A PUPPY.

AWAA! AWAA! MOM!

ONE DAY SCAMP GOT THE ITCH TO GO A-ROAMIN'!...

THAT'S A LOTTA GROWN-UP YAP!

STREET OUT OF BOUNDS FOR PUPPIES!

I'M DIGGIN' OUT, KIDS!

STREET OUT OF BOUNDS FOR PUPPIES!

OH-H-H-H, SCAMP!

IT'S EASY TO RUN AWAY FROM HOME...

STREET OUT OF BOUNDS FOR...

BUT NOT SO EASY TO RUN BACK...

SO WHO'S SCARED?

WHEN LADY AND THE TRAMP COUNTED TAILS AT SUPPERTIME...

...ONE WAS MISSING...

WHERE'S YOUR LITTLE BROTHER SCAMP?

OF COURSE! WHERE HE'S TOLD **NOT** TO GO!

KEEP OFF THE GRASS!

GOOD EVENING, TRAMP. LOST SOMETHING?

OUR LITTLE KID! SCAMP! CAN YOU FOLLOW A TRAIL, TRUSTY?

WELL-NOW-UH-UHH-BIT OF A COLD-ACHEW!

...AND BLOCKS AWAY...

I THINK SCAMP WENT THISAWAY...

SNIF!

MEANWHILE...

LISTEN, TRUSTY! I HEAR SOMETHING!

SNIF!

IT'S A FIGHT, TRUSTY! IT'S SCAMP! COME ON!

POOR LITTLE SCAMP! I MAY NEVER SEE HIM AGAIN.

DON'T CRY, LASSIE. TRAMP WILL FIND HIM.

HE NEVER WAS REALLY NAUGHTY. HE WAS JUST PLAYFUL AND FULL OF BARKS AND... AND ...SWEET!

HIST! I HEAR WHISTLING! IT'S "ROLLIN' HOME"!

THAT CAN ONLY BE TRAMP!

LADY, HERE'S YOUR RUNAWAY SON!

OH, MY PRECIOUS! MY DARLING! YOU'VE BEEN HURT!

A BIT OF A BATTLE WITH A BULLY...BUT I LICKED HIM EASY... SCAMP HELPED...HE'S A CHIP OFF THE OLD BLOCK!

GEE, THANKS, POP!

FIGHTING, FIGHTING, FIGHTING! YOU'RE A FINE FATHER AND SON! NOW GET IN THAT DOGHOUSE, BOTH OF YOU!

THEN LADY SAID, "GET IN THAT DOGHOUSE!" AND SHE HASN'T SPOKEN TO ME SINCE!

THEY'RE A VERRA STRANGE BREED, LADDIE ...WOMEN!

OF COURSE I WAS ANGRY WHEN TRAMP STARTED BRAGGING ABOUT HOW GOOD A FIGHTER HIS OWN SON IS!

I'M AFRAID YOU DON'T SEE THE MALE POINT OF VIEW, MIZ LADY.

WALT DISNEY

WE'RE "JUST PUPPIES" TO THEM! NOBODY UNDERSTANDS US!

The End

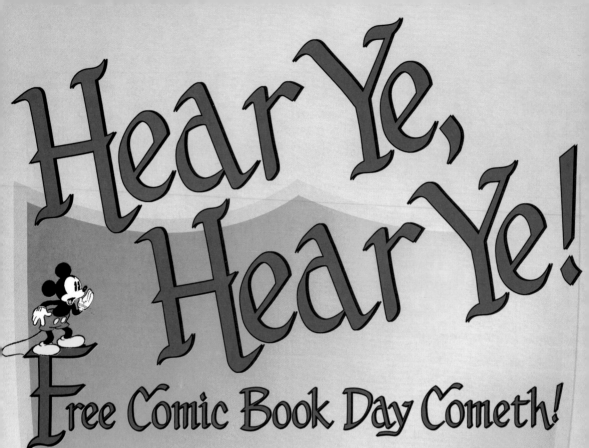

Hear Ye, Hear Ye!

Free Comic Book Day Cometh!

On the 5th Day of May in the Year 2007

Visit your local comic shop to pick up your free Disney comic book featuring

Mickey Mouse
in
The Robin Hood Adventure

by Eisner Awards Hall of Fame Artist

Floyd Gottfredson

GEMSTONE
PUBLISHING

www.gemstonepub.com/disney

WALT DISNEY'S

THE JR WOODCHUCKS

in **Arrested Development**

Keep Our Planet Clean

VERY GOOD, MEN!

GENERALS HUEY, DEWEY AND LOUIE REPORTING FOR *OPERATION TIDY PARK*, RANGER GRANGER!

H 8023

I'M GLAD YOU WOODCHUCKS ARE HELPING TO PROTECT NATURE! ALAS, THERE AREN'T MANY PEOPLE *LEFT* WHO *CARE* ABOUT UNSPOILED NATURAL BEAUTY...

...AND *MONEY TALKS LOUDER* THAN THOSE WHO *DO!* ESPECIALLY WHEN IT COMES TO NATURE PRESERVES!

SO MANY SANCTUARIES HAVE ALREADY BEEN *LOST!* FOLKS AREN'T EXACTLY *BAD*, BUT THEY OFTEN JUST DON'T *RESPECT* NATURE! THEY STREW THEIR *TRASH* ON THE GROUND...

WELL, ENOUGH GLOOM! I MUST ATTEND AN IMPORTANT CITY COUNCIL MEETING! I'LL BE BACK IN AWHILE TO CHECK UP ON YOUR CLEANUP JOB!

RANGER GRANGER SEEMS AWFULLY UPSET ABOUT SOMETHING!

I THINK HE'S *TOO* PESSIMISTIC!

TRUE! NOT *EVERYONE* IS CONCERNED *ENOUGH* ABOUT NATURE...

...BUT PEOPLE AREN'T AS HARD TO REACH AS HE THINKS!

WE'RE AWFULLY *SORRY*, SIR, BUT IT'S ALL THE FAULT OF THAT AWFUL *MAN* SITTING OVER THERE!

YOU SEE WHAT I SEE?

YEAH! RANGER GRANGER LOOKS *RELAXED*... LIKE A *WEIGHT'S* BEEN TAKEN OFF HIS SHOULDERS! MAYBE NATURE'S BEAUTY FINALLY GOT TO HIM!

MR. CLEARCUT PLANS TO TURN THIS FOREST INTO A *GOLF COURSE*, RANGER! HIS CONTRACT'S GONE, BUT HE MIGHT THINK OF SOMETHING ELSE!

LET'S FIRST SEE WHAT WE HAVE UNDER THAT BASKET!

WHAT'S *THAT* ON HIS FACE?

THE CONTRACT!

STUCK TOGETHER WITH *CHEWING GUM*!

WHAT A *HORRIBLE* TWIST OF FATE! WHEN WE HIT THE TREE, HIS *BUBBLE POPPED* AND HELD THE CONTRACT TOGETHER!

⸕HAH!⸕ I *WIN*! TH' BIRDIES AN' BUNNIES HAVE 24 HOURS TO CLEAR OUT! ⸕YEE-HAH!⸕

DON'T GAS UP YOUR BULLDOZERS *YET*!

POP!

OH NO!

WHAT YOU *COULDN'T KNOW* IS HOW TODAY'S *CITY COUNCIL MEETING* CAME OUT! WE VOTED TO *CANCEL* ALL DEVELOPMENT PLANS FOR THIS FOREST! IT SEEMS *SOME* FOLKS *DO* CARE ABOUT NATURE!

HOORAY!

WALT DISNEY'S
The LI'L BAD WOLF

LOOK, SON, IF YOU REALLY WANT TO BE A TRUE-BLUE WOLF OF THE OLD SCHOOL LIKE **ME**, YA GOTTA **WORK** AT IT!

YOU MEAN I HAVE TO PRACTICE, RIGHT, POP?

KJS 001

EGG-**ZACTLY**! IF YOU EVER EXPECT TO KNOCK OVER THAT DOGGONE PRACTICAL PIG'S JOINT, YOU HAVE TO LEARN TO **HUFF** AN' **PUFF**!

BRICK WALLS DON'T COME DOWN WITH NO GENTLE ZEPHYRS, YOU KNOW!

HERE, I'LL SHOW YOU WHAT I MEAN!

BUT THAT'S **OUR** FENCE, POP!

YEP AN' WITH MY HURRICANE-LIKE BREATH I'LL BLOW THE BEJABBERS OUT OF IT! WATCH!

I HUFF... AN' **PUFF**... ...AN'...

FOOF

D 97438

WHOA!

OUCH!

THUD!

THE SPRINGS IN THAT CHAIR MUST BE SHOT! BETTER TRY THE SOFA!

OUCH!!

THUD!

THAT FELT LIKE AN EARTHQUAKE! I'LL JUST SIT AND ROCK AWHILE!

TRIPLE-OUCH!

THUD!

G-G-GYRO? YOU *G-G-GOTTA* GET OVER HERE! MY FURNITURE... *HATES* ME!

REALLY? WHAT DID IT SAY?

NOTHING! BUT I... I...

NOW LET ME SEE! HMMMM...

HMMMM...

HMMMM! I THINK I'VE GOT THE ANSWER!

ALL I NEED IS *THIS!*

AND *THIS!*

HEY!

LEGGO! I *REFUSE* TO BE A GUINEA PIG!

GEE! I THOUGHT HE WAS A DUCK!

SOON —

BUT, GYRO! IS THIS THE *ONLY* SOLUTION?

GYRO GEARLOOSE INVENTOR OF STUFF

AND SO —

GANGWAY! *HERE'S* THE ANSWER TO OUR WOES!

HMPH! *JUST* WHAT WE NEEDED! *ANOTHER* CHAIR!

HEY! GET A LOAD OF *THIS* UGLY THING!

I *MAY* BE UGLY, BUT AT LEAST I'M NOT STUPID!

B-B-BUT I PLAN TO TAKE A NIGHT COURSE! IN COMPUTER PROGRAMMING!

⇒GUFFAW!⇐ GOOD ONE, DUCK-CHAIR!

HAVE YOU COME TO JOIN OUR FIGHT? WE WANT THE SAME RIGHTS AS THE CITIZENS OF DUCKBURG!

NOT *ME*, BROTHER!

WHO NEEDS NASTY STUFF LIKE WORK, SCHOOL AND TAXES?